My Book About Weather

This book helps young children recognize and describe the different kinds of weather they are likely to experience during the year — the sunshine, snow, rain and wind. The book also investigates exceptional weather, such as hurricanes, tornadoes, thunder and lightning, and looks at the climate in hot and cold parts of the world. The simple text aims to teach children the words they need to know to talk about the weather in their immediate surroundings, as well as further afield.

My Book About

The Body

Clothes

Food

Houses and Homes

Toys

Weather

Editor: Anna Girling
Designer: Loraine Hayes

First published in 1991 by
Wayland (Publishers) Ltd
61 Western Road, Hove
East Sussex BN3 1JD, England

British Library Cataloguing in Publication Data
Jackman, Wayne
Weather.
1. Weather
I. Title   II. Series
551.5

ISBN 0 7502 0094 4

Typeset by Kalligraphic Design Ltd, Horley, Surrey
Printed and bound by Casterman S.A., Belgium

Words that are **underlined** in the text
are explained in the glossary on page 22.

My Book About Weather

WAYNE JACKMAN

Wayland

It is the start of a new day. Let's look out of the window.

What is the weather like today? Does it look warm?

Today the sun is shining.
It is shining on this girl.

Do you think she likes the sun?

These children are having a picnic.
What are they eating?

It is fun to have a picnic when it is warm.

There are lots of people
on the beach today.
Look at all the **umbrellas**.
How many can you count?

Sometimes the sunshine is too hot in **summer**.
These umbrellas help to keep people cool.

On some days there are lots of **clouds** in the sky. The weather is dull and it rains.

Can you see the raindrops on the window?

When it rains
we put on
our coats.

This girl has
got red
Wellington
boots.
**Where is
her head
hidden?**

Sometimes it snows in **winter**.
The snow covers everything up
with white **snowflakes**.

Can you see footprints in the snow?

A warm coat and a warm hat will keep you cosy.
Then you can play in the snow.

Look at these huge snowmen.
What are their eyes made from?

Sometimes the weather is very windy.

The wind is blowing these sailing boats along.
The big sails catch the wind.

It is fun to fly a kite when it is windy. The wind lifts the kite off the ground.

What colour is this kite?

After a very hot day there might be a **storm**. The rain pours down.

What noise do raindrops make?

In a storm you see **lightning** and hear **thunder**.

The lightning comes first and then the noisy rumble of thunder.
It sounds like a giant clapping his hands.

Some parts of the world have very bad storms.
These storms are called **hurricanes** or **typhoons**.

The wind is very strong.
A typhoon can blow down buildings.
Sometimes people lose their homes.

A **tornado** is another kind of storm.

The wind blows round and round.
It makes a pointed cloud like this.

Look at this picture.
This is a **flood**.
A flood happens when there
is lots and lots of rain.

How would you get to school in a flood?

This sandy place is a **desert**.
A desert does not get much rain.
Sometimes there is not enough water to drink.

**Do you know where camels keep their water?
Can you guess?**

Some parts of the world are always cold.
It is very cold at the **North Pole**.

Polar bears do not mind the ice and snow.

Some parts of the world are very hot.
In Africa the sun shines much of the time.

This lioness and her cub enjoy sunbathing.
Do you like hot or cold weather best?

Glossary

Clouds The white or grey masses floating in the sky. Rain falls from clouds.

Desert A place where very few plants will grow, usually because there is not enough water.

Flood Lots of water that has spread from a river or the sea on to dry land.

Hurricanes Storms with very strong winds.

Lightning Flashes of light in the sky which happen during a thunderstorm.

North Pole The point at the far north of the Earth.

Snowflakes The tiny pieces of ice that make up snow.

Storm A time of bad weather when there might be lots of rain, wind, thunder and lightning.

Summer The time of the year when the weather is warmest.

Thunder The loud noise you hear after a flash of lightning.

Tornado A bad storm with whirling winds.

Typhoons The name given to bad storms when they happen over the Pacific Ocean, near China.

Umbrella A folding covered framework for protection against the rain or sun.

Winter The time of the year when the weather is coldest.

Books to read

Let's Look At Rain by Jacqueline Dineen (Wayland, 1988)

Let's Look At Sunshine by Constance Milburn (Wayland, 1987)

A Snowy Day, A Stormy Day, A Sunny Day, A Windy Day, (Giraffe Books series) all by Kate Petty (Hodder & Stoughton, 1989)

The Usborne Book of Weather Facts by Anita Ganeri (Usborne, 1987)

Weather (Starting Science series) by Kay Davies and Wendy Oldfield (Wayland, 1990)

What Will The Weather Be Like Today? by Paul Rogers (Orchard Books, 1989)

Picture acknowledgements

The publishers would like to thank the following for providing photographs for this book: Eye Ubiquitous 4 (A. Carroll), 7 (Derek Redfearn), 10 (Derek Redfearn), 21 (Betty Morris); Robert Harding Picture Agency cover; Hutchison Library 16 (J. G. Fuller); Frank Lane Picture Agency 14 (Steve McCutcheon), 17 (David Houdley); Topham Picture Library 5, 8, 18; Tony Stone Worldwide 11, 12, 15; Wayland Picture Library 19; Timothy Woodcock 6, 13; Zefa 9 (S. Roessler), 20 (J. Bennett).

Index